THE AMAZING
SPIDER-MAN

JUMBO
COLORING & ACTIVITY BOOK

BENDON

BENDON Publishing Int'l., Inc.
Ashland, OH 44805
www.bendonpub.com

Secret Message!

DOCTOR OCTOPUS

Cross out the words DOCTOR OCTOPUS every time you see them in the box. When you reach a letter that does not belong, write it in the circles below to spell the secret words!

DOCTOROCTOPUSODOCT
OROCTOPUSTDOCTOROC
TOPUSTDOCTOROCTOPUS
ODOCTOROCTOPUSODOCT
OROCTOPUSCDOCTOROC
TOPUSTDOCTOROCTOPUS
ADOCTOROCTOPUSVDOCT
OROCTOPUSIDOCTOROCT
OPUSUDOCTOROCTOPUSS

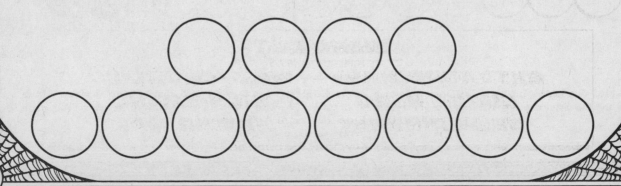

Cross Patch!

Using the words from the list, complete the cross patch puzzle.

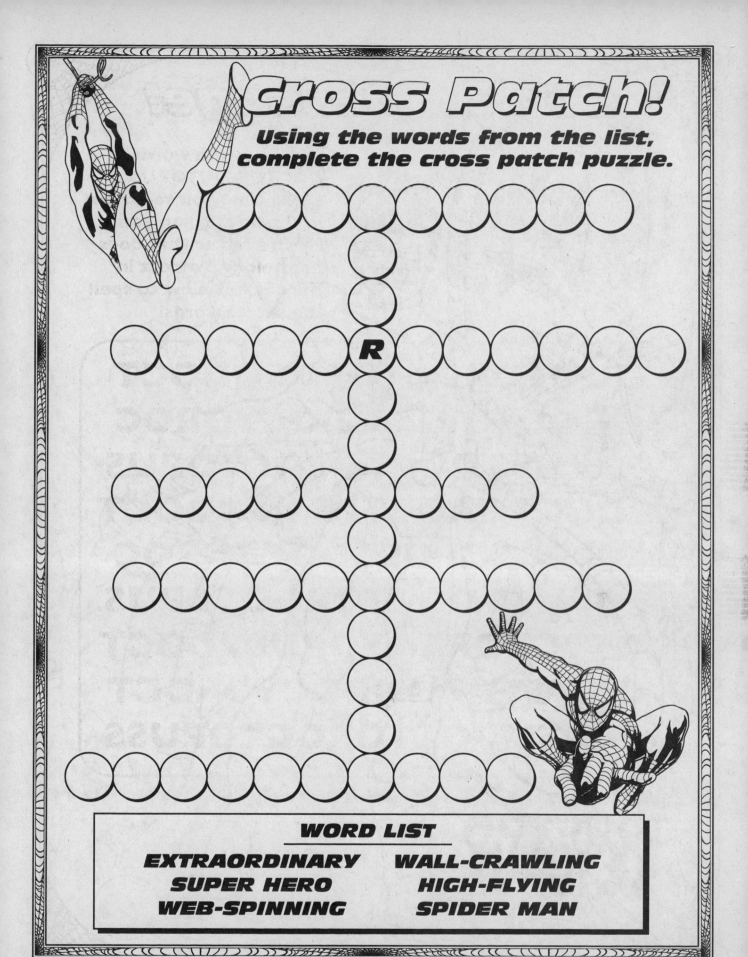

WORD LIST

EXTRAORDINARY   WALL-CRAWLING

SUPER HERO   HIGH-FLYING

WEB-SPINNING   SPIDER MAN

DOCTOR OCTOPUS

Which 2 are EXACTLY the SAME?

Look at the four pictures. Two of them are exactly alike. Can you find them?

1.

2.

3.

4.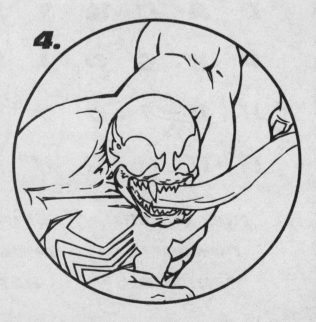

Answers: Numbers 2 and 3.

FIND THE WORDS

```
S T R E N G T H O P E
A V A S P R C H E A K
O L U F R E W O P R I
R A P V A C H B Q K L
E J K R D C B G N E R
H Z A C I R Y O W R E
R U E M A K V B S J D
E A Q W T V I L R C I
P X S P I N N I N G P
U U I O O R T N Z A S
S R H G N I L W A R C
```

HOB GOBLIN	**SPINNING**	**CRAWLING**
POWERFUL	**SPIDER-LIKE**	**SUPER HERO**
RADIATION	**PARKER**	**STRENGTH**

Follow the Path

Using the letters in order from the word

VENOM

follow the correct path to find your way through the maze!

Word Scramble

Using the words from the list, unscramble the letters to correctly spell the names and words!

RHEERPUOS _____

NEGRTTHS _____

REWDIEPBS _____

KCCALABT _____

ROADRITNAXRYE _____

RBEIDTEIPS _____

WORD LIST

SPIDER BITE	**BLACK CAT**
STRENGTH	**EXTRAORDINARY**
SPIDER WEB	**SUPER HERO**

SPIDER-SQUARES

Taking turns, connect a line from one face to another. Whoever makes the line that completes a box puts their initials inside the box. The person with the most squares at the end of the game wins!

EXAMPLE:

Which Piece is MISSING?

Only one of the puzzle pieces below will fit. Can you find the missing piece and complete the puzzle?

A.

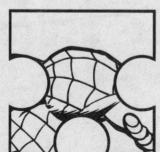

B.

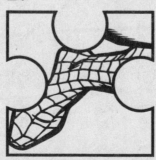

C.

TIC-TAC-TOE

USE THESE SPACES TO CHALLENGE YOUR FAMILY AND FRIENDS!

WHICH SPIDER-MAN IS

DIFFERENT?

One SPIDER-MAN below is an imposter. Can you find the one that is different from the others?

1.

2.

3.

4.

WHO is WHO?

Match the pictures of the villains by writing the correct letter below each close-up!

 **A.**

 **B.**

 **C.**

 **D.**

 **1.** ◯

 **2.** ◯

 **3.** ◯

 **4.** ◯

 **5.** ◯

 **6.** ◯

 **7.** ◯

 **8.** ◯

Answers: 1:C, 2:D, 3:B, 4:A, 5:B, 6:D, 7:A, 8:C

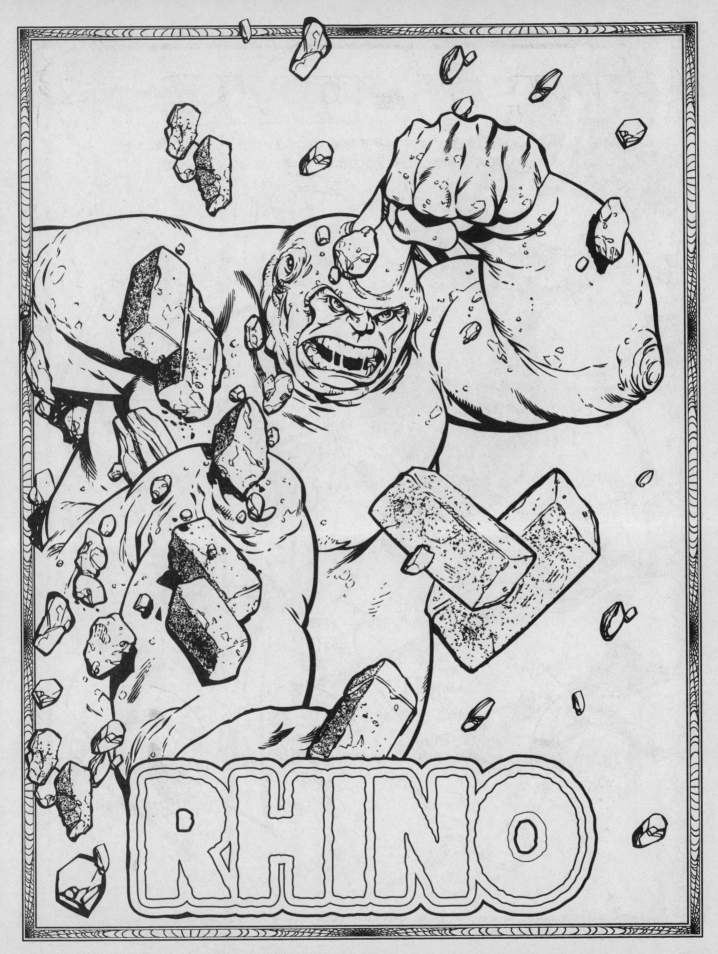

RHINO

SPIDEY MAZE

Help the Amazing Spider-Man
get through the maze and
capture Sandman!

START ▼

FINISH ▼

FIND THE WORDS

```
R  S  C  I  T  E  L  H  T  A  Y
F  Q  T  B  A  O  E  M  Z  I  T
E  B  U  R  G  L  E  R  M  J  I
L  W  T  L  E  C  N  R  Q  R  L
I  Q  A  P  U  N  O  S  A  O  I
C  Y  C  Y  M  F  G  O  L  A  G
I  S  K  X  S  I  R  T  E  K  A
A  M  C  N  X  A  L  E  H  L  C
Z  X  A  C  P  C  L  A  W  S  Z
P  R  L  Q  G  M  K  S  D  O  A
T  X  B  V  W  Z  R  Y  M  T  P
```

BLACK CAT   **AGILITY**   **BURGLER**

FELICIA   **STRENGTH**   **TRANSFORM**

POWERFUL   **CLAWS**   **ATHLETIC**

TIC-TAC-TOE

USE THESE SPACES TO CHALLENGE YOUR FAMILY AND FRIENDS!

SPIDER-SENSE
PUZZLE

Using the list below, unscramble the letters of the words.
Fill in the numbered letters in the spaces at the bottom to create a new word!

WORD LIST

AMAZING	SPIDER WEB	PROTECTOR
STRENGTH	SPIDER BITE	

ENGRTTHS _____ _____ _____ _____ _____ _____ _____ _____
                              10.   5.

REDBIITPES _____ _____ _____ _____ _____ _____ _____ _____ _____ _____
                                        3.   9.

ECTTOORRP _____ _____ _____ _____ _____ _____ _____ _____ _____
                        6.   7.   2.

REDWIEPBS _____ _____ _____ _____ _____ _____ _____ _____ _____
                                                      8.

ZAMIANG _____ _____ _____ _____ _____ _____ _____
                      4.   1.

1.	2.	3.	4.	5.	6.	7.	8.	9.	10.

FIND THE WORDS

```
Z S G E N I U S V R E
L T J G X C R U E P V
P C E Z Q E O P K B I
S R X N C G H O V E L
U I T S T V W T N M M
I M R Q C A J C K Y I
V I Y R O T C O D K N
A N A M R K P L U Q D
T A Z Q E L Z S E U O
C L S E G N O R T S P
O Q T K I T E R C Y R
```

DOCTOR	TENTACLES	STRONG
OCTOPUS	ENEMY	EVIL MIND
OCTAVIUS	GENIUS	CRIMINAL

Finish the Picture!
Spider-Man is fighting a dangerous battle! Draw your own version of a villain.

BLACK CAT PUZZLE

Have a parent or care-giver cut out the puzzle pieces on the dotted lines.

Mix up the pieces, and put the picture back together!

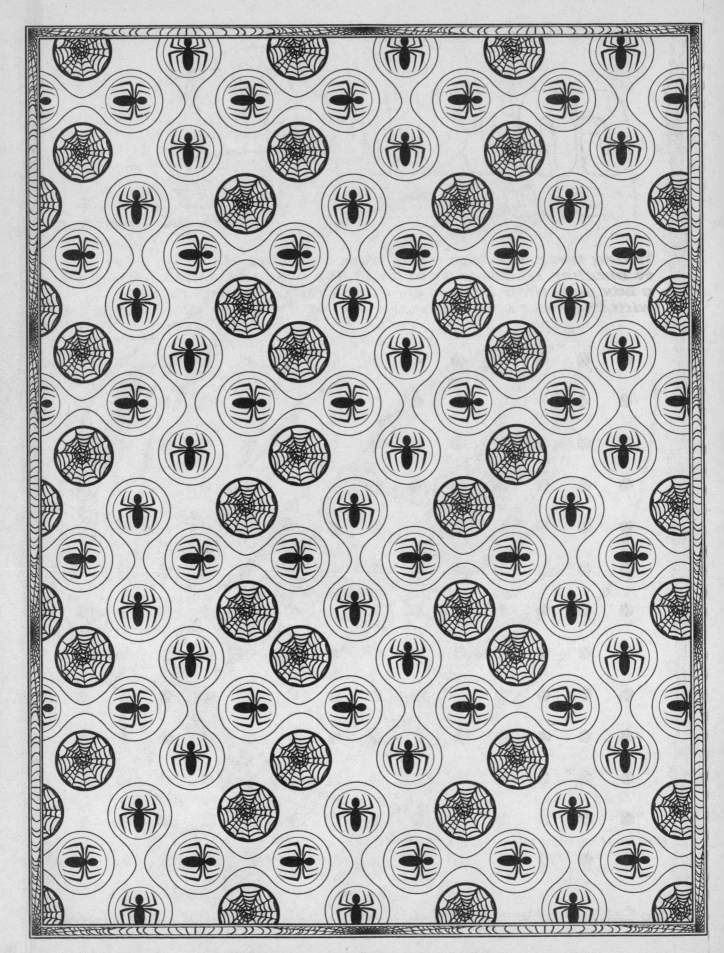

GOBLIN SQUARES

Taking turns, connect a line from one pumpkin to another. Whoever makes the line that completes a box puts their initials inside the box. The person with the most squares at the end of the game wins!

EXAMPLE:

Follow the Path

Using the letters in order from the word
BLACK CAT
follow the correct path to find your way through the maze!

FIND THE WORDS

```
S D R W C O N N E R S
U T V D R A Z I L E P
J R N O P E T Y U P I
T A M E L Q B W F T S
E N C W M E C O R I O
W S A J G I R F E L A
M F C M S M R I W E B
Z O G H U C H E O L T
B R T L J H L T P O P
X M A Q V I N G Y X R
E B R A G I L I T Y E
```

LIZARD   **TRANSFORM**   **POWERFUL**

CONNERS   **INHUMAN**   **EXPERIMENT**

REPTILE   **AGILITY**   **FORMULA**

WHO is WHO?

Match the pictures of the faces by writing the correct letter below each close-up!

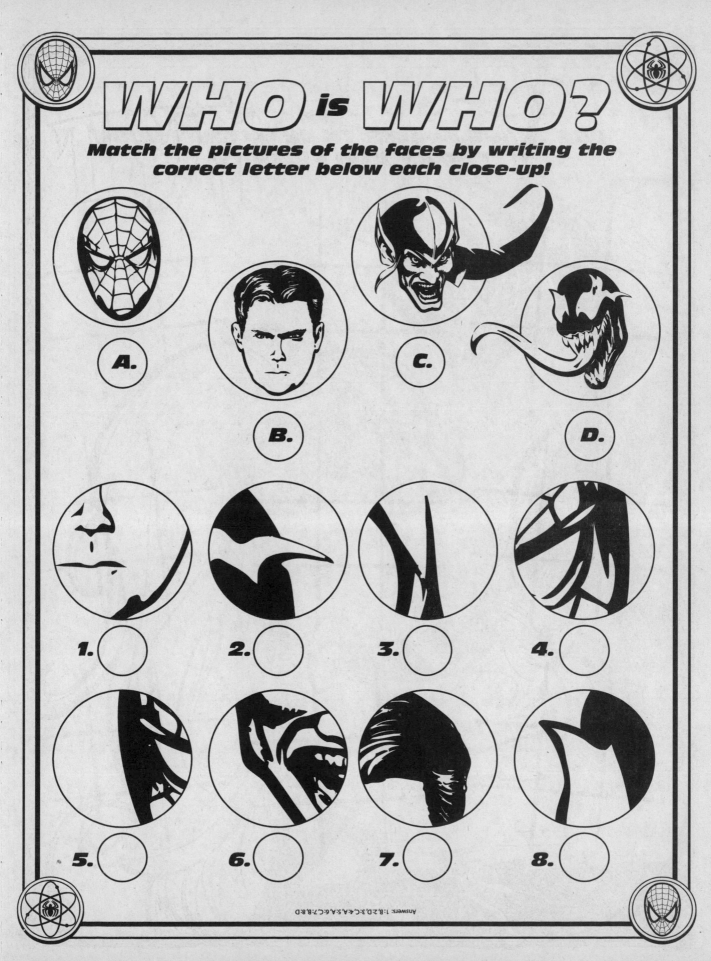

A.

B.

C.

D.

1.

2.

3.

4.

5.

6.

7.

8.

TIC-TAC-TOE

USE THESE SPACES TO CHALLENGE YOUR FAMILY AND FRIENDS!

ELECTRO SQUARES

EXAMPLE:

Taking turns, connect a line from one lightning bolt to another. Whoever makes the line that completes a box puts their initials inside the box. The person with the most squares at the end of the game wins!

Word Scramble

Using the words from the list, unscramble the letters to correctly spell the names and words!

RLEIDKIESP _____

LFYHGIINGH _____

EBLECNNU _____

INPNSIBNEGW _____

TMNAUYA _____

YJRAANME _____

WORD LIST

UNCLE BEN	**SPIDER-LIKE**
AUNT MAY	**HIGH-FLYING**
MARY JANE	**WEB-SPINNING**

Secret Message!

Cross out the words VENOM every time you see them in the box. When you reach a letter that does not belong, write it in the circles below to spell the secret words!

VENOMEVENOMDVENOM
VENOMVENOMDVENOM
VENOMIVENOMVENOME
VENOMVENOMBVENOM
VENOMRVENOMVENOM
VENOMVENOMOVENOM
VENOMCVENOMVENOM
VENOMVENOMVENOM
VENOMVENOMKVENOM

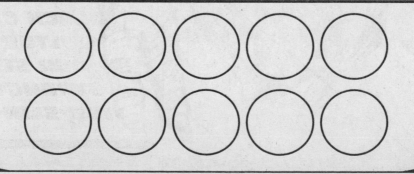

Cross Patch!

Using the words from the list, complete the cross patch puzzle.

E

WORD LIST

SPIDER BITE
BLACK CAT
VULTURE
SPIDER SENSE
STRENGTH
WEB-SLINGER

WHICH DOCTOR OCTOPUS IS
DIFFERENT?

**One DOCTOR OCTOPUS below is an imposter.
Can you find the one that is different
from the others?**

1.

2.

3.

4.

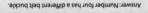

Answer: Number four has a different belt buckle.

Finish the Picture!

Finish drawing a city below Spider-Man as he races to fight crime!

FIND THE WORDS

M K U R E T S I N I S

J E T H C I T R W H B

L I N V E N T O R X M

Y S A G E G N E V E R

O A I R I W T Q U S V

T V L C M N B L L D I

H P L A B O E C T R L

G A I R C M T E U Y L

I O R E W O P N R B A

L P B V C W K U E V I

F R M R U R C L B I N

VULTURE **SINISTER** **REVENGE**

ENGINEER **POWER** **BRILLIANT**

INVENTOR **FLIGHT** **VILLAIN**

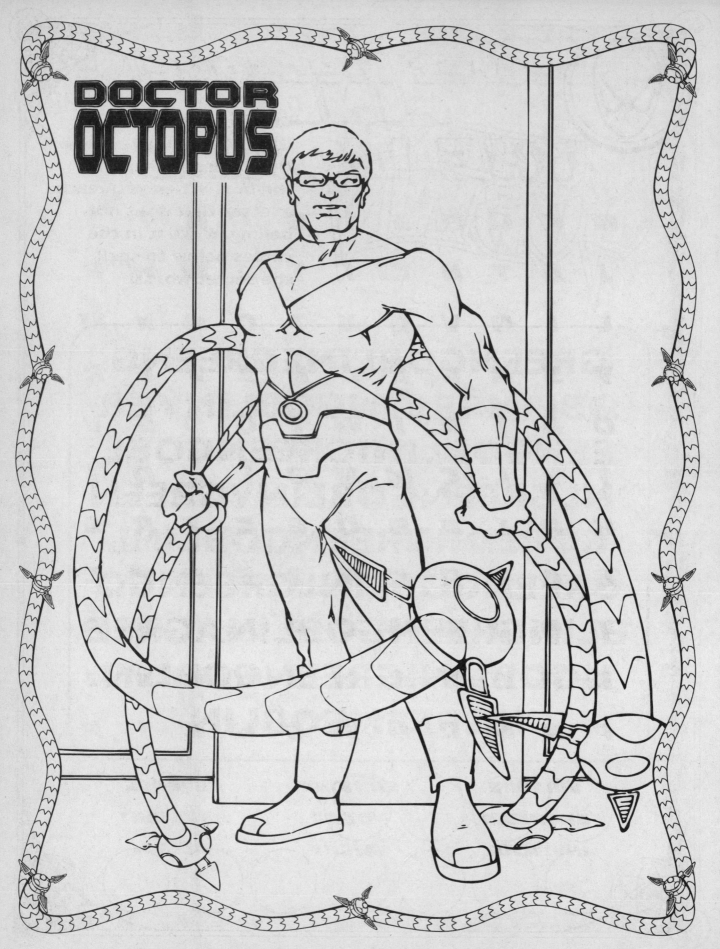

DOCTOR OCTOPUS

Cross out the words GREEN GOBLIN every time you see them in the box. When you reach a letter that does not belong, write it in the circles below to spell the secret words!

GREENGOBLINEGREENG
OBLINGREENGOBLINVGR
EENGOBLINIGREENGOBL
INLGREENGOBLINVGREEN
GOBLINIGREENGOBLINL
GREENGOBLINLGREENGO
BLINGREENGOBLINAGREE
NGOBLINIGREENGOBLIN
NGREENGOBLIN

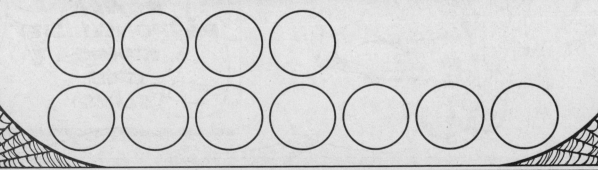

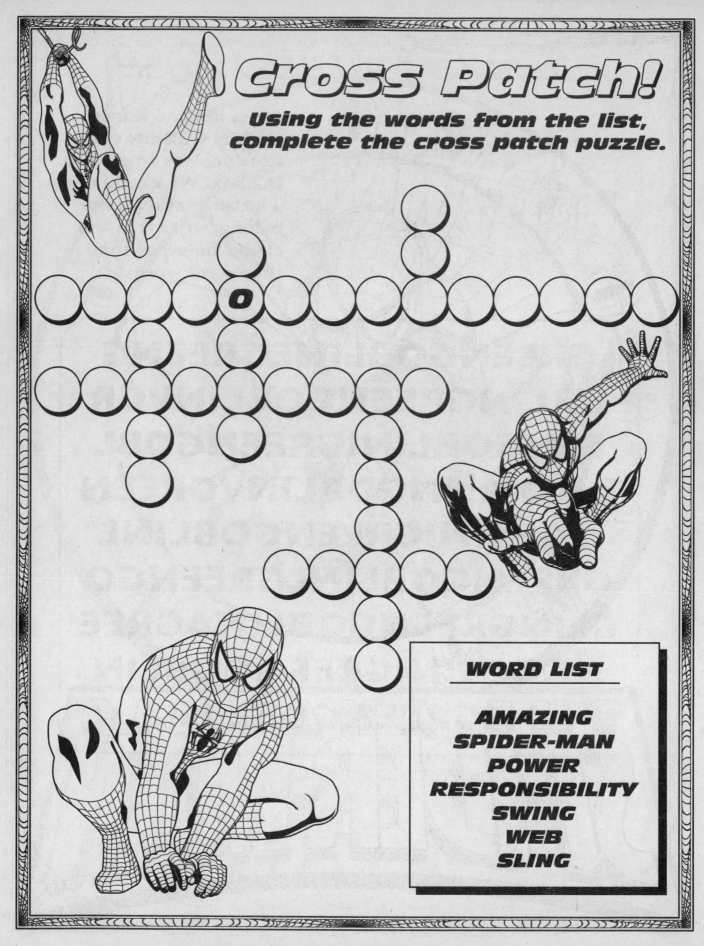

Cross Patch!

Using the words from the list, complete the cross patch puzzle.

O

WORD LIST

AMAZING
SPIDER-MAN
POWER
RESPONSIBILITY
SWING
WEB
SLING

WHICH SPIDER-MAN IS
DIFFERENT?

**One Spider-Man below is an imposter.
Can you find the one that is different
from the others?**

1.

2.

3.

4.

Answer: The spider on number four's chest has only seven legs.

Which 2 are EXACTLY the SAME?

Look at the four pictures. Two of them are exactly alike. Can you find them?

1.

2.

3.

4.

Answers: Numbers 1 and 4.

Finish the Picture!
Finish drawing Spider-Man as he swings across the city!

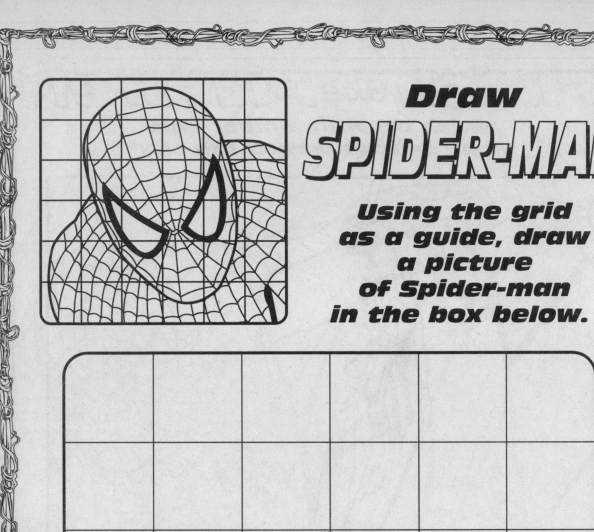

Draw
SPIDER-MAN

Using the grid as a guide, draw a picture of Spider-man in the box below.

How Many Words?

How many words can you make by using the letters in

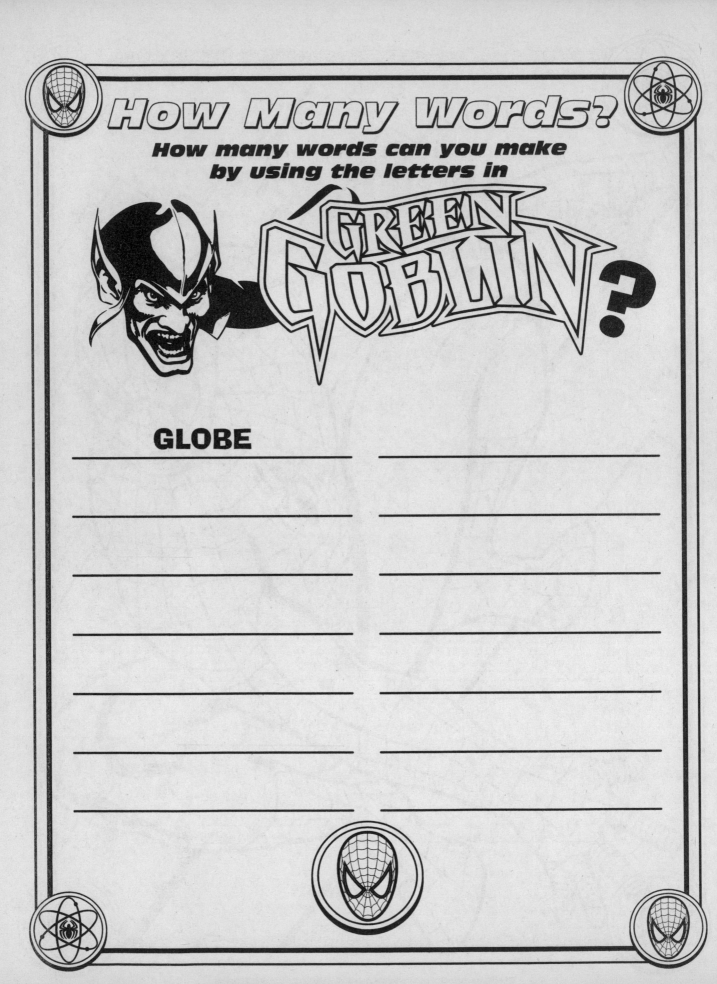

GREEN GOBLIN?

GLOBE

_____   _____

_____   _____

_____   _____

_____   _____

_____   _____

_____   _____

Word Scramble

Using the words from the list, unscramble the letters to correctly spell the names of Spider-Man's foes!

KCCLB AAT ___ ___ ___ ___ ___ ___ ___ ___

NOEMV ___ ___ ___ ___ ___

NRAAGCE ___ ___ ___ ___ ___ ___ ___

DMNAANS ___ ___ ___ ___ ___ ___ ___

IHNRO ___ ___ ___ ___ ___

AZRIDL ___ ___ ___ ___ ___ ___

CTERLOE ___ ___ ___ ___ ___ ___ ___

UTLRUEV ___ ___ ___ ___ ___ ___ ___

RHINO	SANDMAN	VENOM
LIZARD	ELECTRO	CARNAGE
	BLACK CAT	VULTURE

SPIDEY-SQUARES

Taking turns, connect a line from one spider to another. Whoever makes the line that completes a box puts their initials inside the box.
The person with the most squares at the end of the game wins!

EXAMPLE:

TIC-TAC-TOE

USE THESE SPACES TO CHALLENGE YOUR FAMILY AND FRIENDS!

Have a parent or care-giver cut out the puzzle pieces on the dotted lines. Mix up the pieces, and put the picture back together!

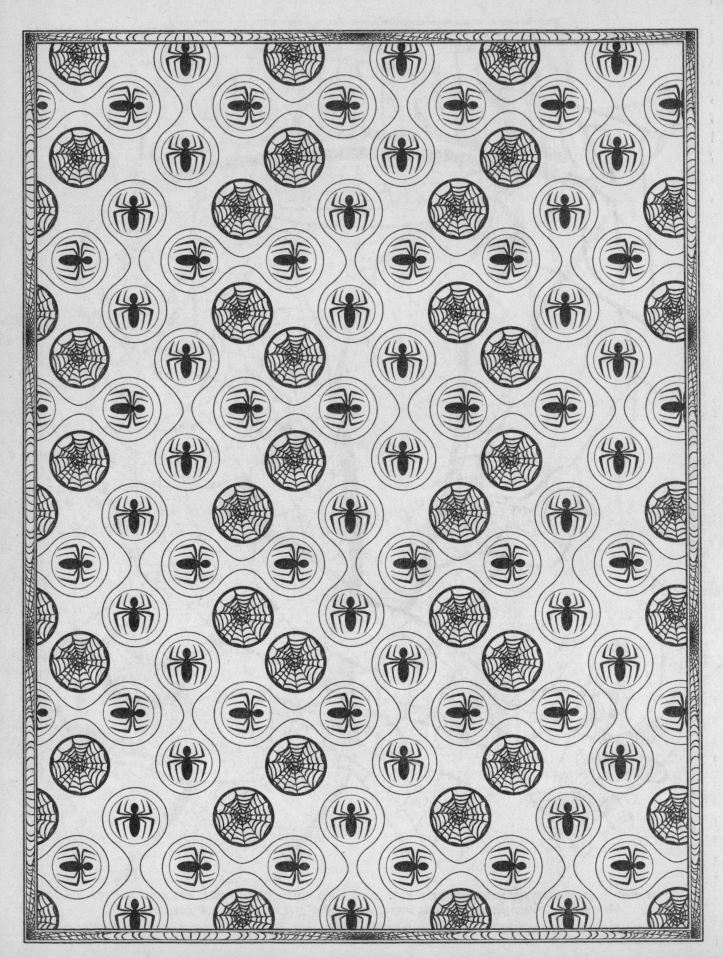

PETER PARKER

IS

THE AMAZING
SPIDER-MAN

WHICH SPIDER-MAN IS
DIFFERENT?

One SPIDER-MAN below is an imposter. Can you find the one that is different from the others?

1.

2.

3.

4.

Answer: The finger on number two is different.

Which Piece is MISSING?

Only one of the puzzle pieces below will fit. Can you find the missing piece and complete the puzzle?

A. **B.** **C.**

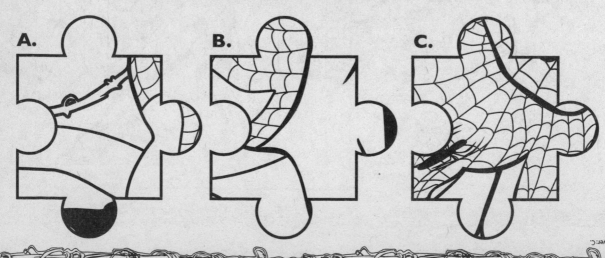

SPIDEY MAZE

Help the Amazing Spider-Man get through the maze and capture Doctor Octopus!

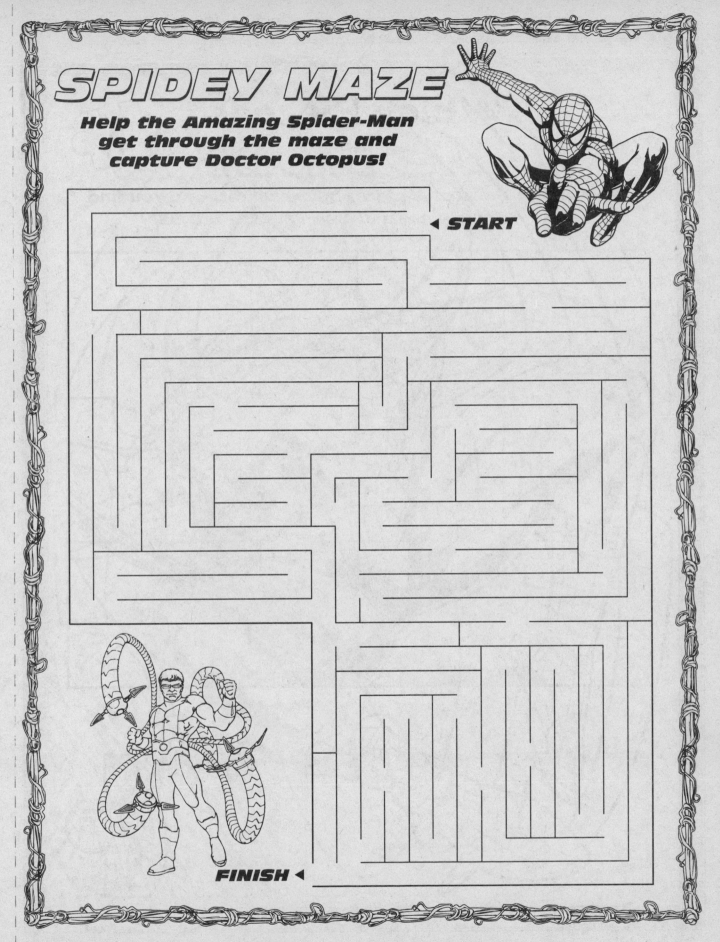

◄ START

FINISH ◄

Finish the Picture!
Finish drawing the scene as Spider-Man keeps watch over the city!

WHO is WHO?

Match the letters by the villians to the the correct names!

 **A.**

 **B.**

 **C.**

 **D.**

 **E.**

 **F.**

 **G.**

○ BLACK CAT

○ VENOM

○ CARNAGE

○ SANDMAN

○ GREEN GOBLIN

○ DOCTOR OCTOPUS

○ RHINO

Answers from the top: D,F,C,E,A,B,G

SPIDER-SENSE

PUZZLE

Using the list below, unscramble the letters of the words.
Fill in the numbered letters in the spaces at the bottom to create a new word!

WORD LIST

| SPIDER-MAN | VENOM | BLACK CAT |
| CARNAGE | OCTOPUS |

MREANIPDS _____ _____ _____ _____ _____ _____ _____ _____ _____
                          1.   2.

OTPCUOS _____ _____ _____ _____ _____ _____ _____
                    7.   8.

CCKAATLB _____ _____ _____ _____ _____   _____ _____ _____
                                                              4.

ONEMV _____ _____ _____ _____ _____
                          3.

NRAGAEC _____ _____ _____ _____ _____ _____ _____
                6.   9.   5.

1.	2.	3.	4.	5.	6.	7.	8.	9.

FIND THE WORDS

```
S A N D M A N A L O
X P Q R V L G T S V
Z O I W E I N T V I
E R E D V Z I A I L
R T G W E A Z C C L
U C A A N R A K R A
T E N N O D M C H I
L L R J M V A A I N
U E A S T R O L N X
V B C Q N I L B O G
```

SPIDER-MAN	LIZARD	BLACK CAT
AMAZING	ELECTRO	CARNAGE
VILLAIN	VULTURE	VENOM
GOBLIN	RHINO	SANDMAN

FIND THE WORDS

```
S A T A C K C A L B
G H Q E S Z Y P K B
N N S G U V O R W N
I A F N P A Z O H O
Y M W I E G Y T H I
L R B L R C G E J T
F E U W H N A C X A
H D I A E T R T V I
G I M R R H Z O D D
I P T C O J O R A A
H S P I N N I N G R
```

SUPER HERO   **SPIDER-MAN**   **SPINNING**

BLACK CAT   **RADIATION**   **CRAWLING**

STRENGTH   **PROTECTOR**   **HIGH-FLYING**

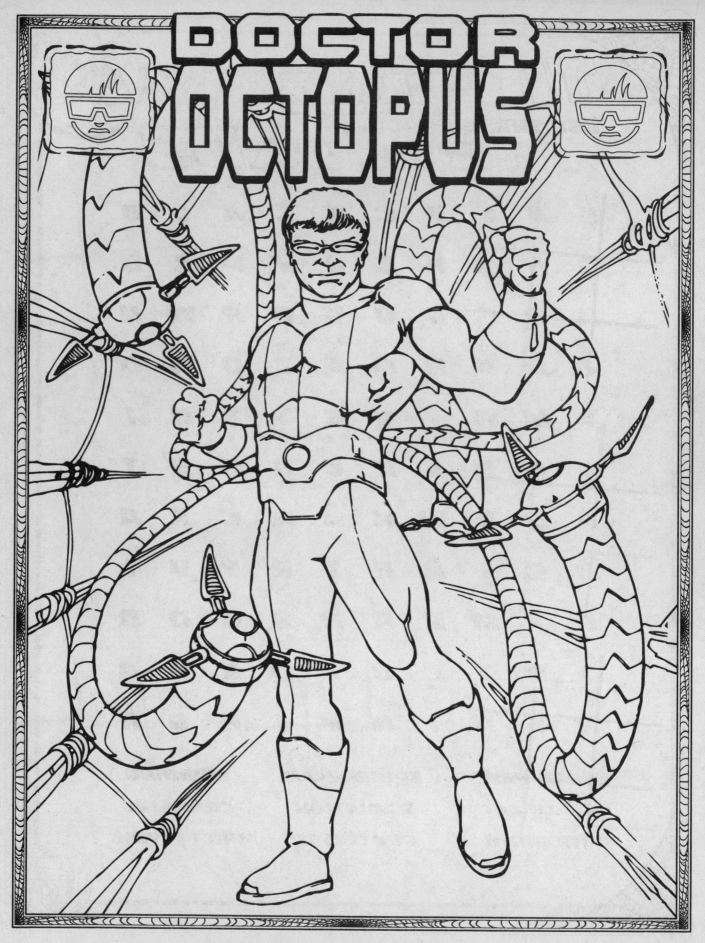

TIC-TAC-TOE

USE THESE SPACES TO CHALLENGE YOUR FAMILY AND FRIENDS!

SPIDER-SQUARES

Taking turns, connect a line from one face to another. Whoever makes the line that completes a box puts their initials inside the box. The person with the most squares at the end of the game wins!

EXAMPLE:

WHICH WAY?

Which way should Spider-Man go to reach the Lizard?

START

FINISH

FIND THE WORDS

```
S U E S R E W O P A
P P T R Q Z B C E W
I G I A H J W V T M
D W B D R T U O E A
E Y R I E O N P R R
R A E A C R C S P Y
M M D T L A L T A J
A T I I D V E I R A
N N P O E Y B X K N
R U S N A P E X E E
A A B R X T N V R E
```

SPIDER-LIKE   **PETER PARKER**   **SPIDER-MAN**

MARY JANE   **POWER**   **UNCLE BEN**

RADIATION   **SPIDER BITE**   **AUNT MAY**

WHICH VENOM IS

DIFFERENT?

One VENOM below is an imposter. Can you find the one that is different from the others?

1.

2.

3.

4.

Answer: Venom number three has a different grin.

Finish the Picture!

Finish drawing the

Lizard

Crack the Code!

Use the code below to fill in the blanks and reveal the secret words!

__ __ __ __ __   __ __ __ __ __ __
8. 24. 10. 24. 9.   8. 26. 9. 21. 24. 9.

__ __ __ __ __   __ __ __
16. 7. 25. 6. 24.   1. 24. 7.

__ __ __ __   __ __ __
26. 16. 7. 10.   20. 26. 14.

__ __ __ __   __ __ __ __
20. 26. 9. 14.   5. 26. 7. 24.

__
__ __ __ __ __ __   __ __ __ __
17. 8. 22. 2. 24. 9.   6. 22. 21. 24.

1.	2.	3.	4.	5.	6.	7.	8.	9.	10.	11.
B	D	F	H	J	L	N	P	R	T	V

12.	13.	14.	15.	16.	17.	18.	19.	20.	21.	22.
X	Z	Y	W	U	S	Q	O	M	K	I

23.	24.	25.	26.
G	E	C	A

Secret Message!

Cross out the words **SPIDER-MAN** every time you see them in the box. When you reach a letter that does not belong, write it in the circles below to spell the secret words!

SPIDERMANGSPIDERMANS
PIDERMANRSPIDERMANSP
IDERMANESPIDERMANASPI
DERMANTSPIDERMANSPID
ERMANPSPIDERMANSPIDE
RMANOSPIDERMANSPIDER
MANWSPIDERMANESPIDER
MANSPIDERMANSPIDERMA
NSPIDERMANRSPIDERMAN

Crack the Code!

Use the code below to fill in the blanks and reveal the secret words!

___ ___ ___ ___ ___ ___ ___ ___ ___ ___ ___ ___ ___ ___
9. 24. 17. 8. 19. 7. 17. 22. 1. 22. 6. 22. 10. 14.

___ ___ ___ ___ ___ ___ ___
26. 20. 26. 13. 22. 7. 23.

___ ___ ___ ___ ___   ___ ___ ___ ___ ___ ___
23. 9. 24. 24. 7.   23. 19. 1. 6. 22. 7.

___ ___ ___ ___ ___ ___   ___ ___ ___ ___ ___ ___ ___
2. 19. 25. 10. 19. 9.   19. 25. 10. 19. 8. 16. 17.

___ ___ ___ ___ ___ ___   ___ ___ ___ ___ ___
17. 8. 22. 2. 24. 9.   17. 24. 7. 17. 24.

1.	2.	3.	4.	5.	6.	7.	8.	9.	10.	11.
B	D	F	H	J	L	N	P	R	T	V

12.	13.	14.	15.	16.	17.	18.	19.	20.	21.	22.
X	Z	Y	W	U	S	Q	O	M	K	I

23.	24.	25.	26.
G	E	C	A

WITH GREAT POWER· ·COMES GREAT RESPONSIBILITY·

PETER PARKER

IS

THE AMAZING SPIDER-MAN

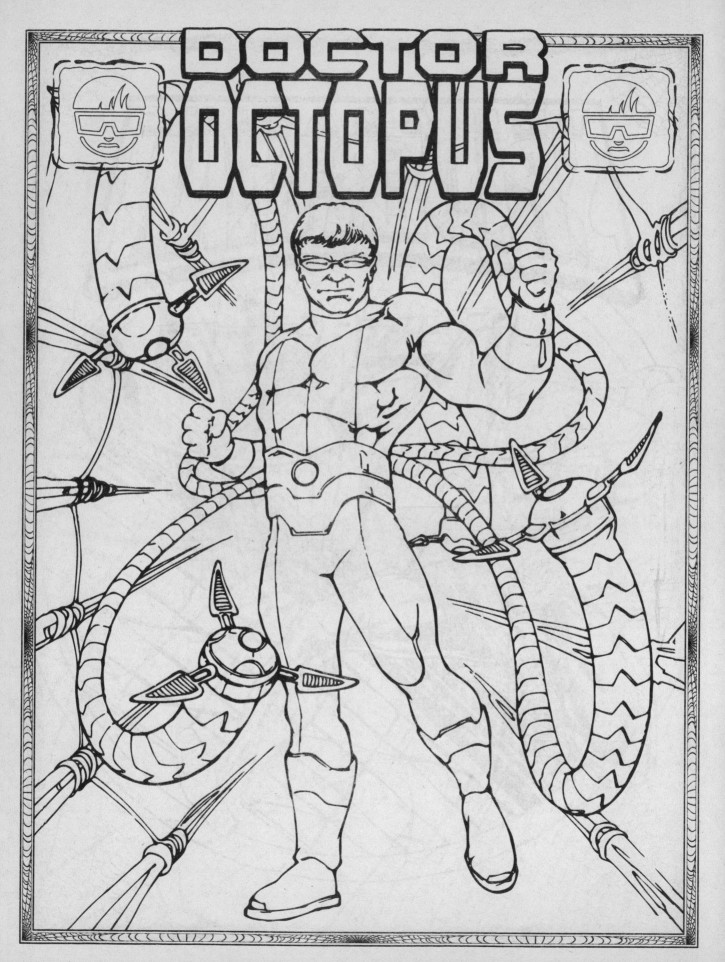

DOCTOR OCTOPUS

AUNT MAY
AUNT MAY
AUNT MAY
AUNT MAY
AUNT MAY
AUNT MAY
AUNT MAY
AUNT MAY
AUNT MAY
AUNT MAY
AUNT MAY
AUNT MAY
AUNT MAY
AUNT MAY